DIGBY—T
DOG IN T

ALAN L. FENNELL

Illustrated with black and white photographs

PAN BOOKS LTD: LONDON

First published 1973 by Pan Books Ltd,
33 Tothill Street, London SW1

ISBN 0 330 23834 5

*Printed and bound in England by
Hazell Watson & Viney Ltd
Aylesbury, Bucks*

Contents

Chapter One

DIGBY'S ADVENTURES BEGIN

The particular dog's home that young Billy White had been visiting was small, for it was in a quiet part of the country, but as far as Billy was concerned, the size didn't matter. The important thing about the home was the occupant of one of the kennels.

Every day for a week, Billy had been visiting the same kennel, and at last he had managed to persuade his mother and grandfather that their house was *not* too small for the thing that mattered most in Billy's life.

Digby was certainly a splendid animal. As Billy walked past the line of kennels he mused over his choice of pet. The other dogs were nice enough, but they did not compare with the fluffy haired Old English Sheepdog that seemed to open its mouth into a broad grin every time Billy came past its pen.

For Billy, one hurdle had been climbed. The

grown-ups at home had accepted that Digby could become a member of the family. But still one problem remained. Within the next five minutes the solution to that problem would become clear – one way or another.

Billy entered the small office and looked up at the sympathetic dog's home manager.

'Does your father know you want the dog?' the man asked, as he glanced at a clock on the wall. It showed the time to be two minutes to three.

'I haven't got a father, sir. He died.' Billy answered flatly. 'Can I take Digby now?'

The manager glanced at the clock again and shook his head slowly. 'I promised a lady she had until three o'clock to make up her mind.'

At that moment, Billy's heart sank as he heard the purring engine of a big limousine arriving outside the office. A chauffeur carrying an armful of assorted dogs followed a stout, over-dressed woman up the pathway. Billy felt the tears welling into his eyes as he imagined Digby becoming part of the woman's menagerie.

Behind Billy, the all-knowing manager shot out a hand and turned the hands of the clock. They jumped a full three minutes.

'I've come for the dog,' announced the woman haughtily.

'I'm sorry, Madam,' smiled the manager indicating the clock which now showed three minutes after three o'clock. 'You're too late. It's been sold to Mr White.'

Billy could hardly believe his ears. At first he wasn't quite sure who Mr White was . . . then he realized *his* name was White.

'Well, really!' snapped the outraged woman, and she turned on her heel and marched off to her car, the straight-faced chauffeur secretly rejoicing at the news.

Five minutes later, Billy was skipping and dancing down the road towards the fields. Ahead of him, at the end of a brand new leash was Digby, his shaggy mane bouncing over his big eyes as he pranced along, as delighted as his young new owner.

Without doubt this was the happiest day in Billy's life.

Not very far from where Billy and Digby were romping across the fields was located a top security NATO Research Establishment. Typical of many such enclosed areas, the base was manned by a collection of top research scientists and guarded by an army of military personnel.

One thing about the centre was not typical – the

presence of a young, handsome man named Jeff Eldon.

Jeff was recognized as the Establishment's Animal Psychologist and because of his special gift with the many and varied animals required for the research programmes, was considered to be a very important part of the base. At the same time, Jeff's happy-go-lucky attitude and his ability to be for ever in trouble with the authorities at the centre, marked him as a man to provide a lot of headaches for the head of security, Colonel Robert Masters.

One of Jeff's special friends was a young lady who insisted on climbing flagpoles, hurling fruit and generally making a nuisance of herself. Her name was Clarissa and she was a highly intelligent, if boisterous chimpanzee.

It was a rather special day at the establishment, for General Frank, a high-ranking NATO officer, was due to arrive to be briefed on the results of an exciting research project. Clarissa liked nothing better than to upset high-ranking officers, in particular Colonel Masters, and she chose this moment to escape Jeff's clutches and reach the roof of the administration block.

'Clarissa!' called Jeff, 'Come down. Here look! Lunch!'

In an upper office, Doctor Harz, newly arrived Head of the Psychiatric Section, glanced out of the window and watched Jeff as he tried to coax Clarissa down with a juicy tomato. Harz was intrigued. He had no idea of Clarissa's antics on the roof above his head and imagined Jeff was the first interesting case of insanity he would have to deal with in his new job.

'Well, I'm sure you'll like it here.' Doctor Harz's attention was drawn back to the other people in the office. Professor Jameson, Chief Scientist, was trying to complete the introduction of Harz to Colonel Masters. 'We're one big happy family, eh, Masters?'

Meanwhile, the tomato thrown up to Clarissa had been caught by the chimp and duly thrown back at Jeff, to land squarely and squashily on his nose. Jeff tried another titbit: this time a large, firm orange. The fruit spiralled up from his hand, fell short of Clarissa's groping fingers, and crashed through the glass, just as Colonel Masters smiled a welcome at Harz.

Leaping to the shattered window, Colonel Masters was just in time to hear Jeff shouting, 'Come down, darling.'

A split second later, Jeff took in the situation. 'Not you, Colonel,' he apologized with a winning smile. 'It's Clarissa . . . she's on the roof.'

'Well get her down at once. The General will be here at any moment,' thundered the pompous security man, before turning back to impress upon Doctor Harz how efficiently he conducted his responsibilities.

'Is he – all right?' Harz was asking Jameson. 'You know . . .?'

'I know,' sighed Jameson, understanding the doctor's inference. 'He's marvellous with animals, but a little prone to accidents.'

Harz returned to the window where Jeff could still be seen making ape-like gestures and grimaces at Clarissa. 'To throw an orange through a window,' the doctor muttered to himself. 'A rock I perhaps understand – but an *orange*? I should like to spend some time with this man. Observing him maybe.'

Ten minutes later, the key staff at the research centre were lined up in the forecourt of the administration block awaiting the arrival of General Frank.

'Everyone here?' fussed Jameson. Then he saw Jeff Eldon and Clarissa. The animal man had succeeded in getting the chimp off the roof only to have her escape his clutches once again . . . this time up the centrally positioned flag pole. 'Eldon, what the devil are you doing here with the chimp?'

'I thought she'd like to meet the General,' laughed Jeff, managing to grab the chattering ape. 'She's a social climber! She's not bad up flag poles either!'

Jameson caught sight of the General's limousine. 'Keep her in line, Eldon – or else,' he snapped, and strode forward to greet the large American who was supreme chief of the NATO establishments in the area.

As General Frank and Jameson exchanged greetings, Jeff waved a banana at Clarissa, enticing her to get in line with the other research staff. At the last minute, Jeff put the banana in his pocket, hoping the chimp would be intrigued enough to remain quiet, but Clarissa had other ideas. She reached up and withdrew the fruit.

The General was approaching as Jeff snatched back the banana, but Colonel Masters standing to attention suddenly broke rank and grabbed the titbit from Eldon's hand.

'Give *me* that,' he snarled. 'And keep that animal under control.'

'You know Colonel Masters I presume?' Jameson said as the General offered his hand to the security man.

Masters thrust his hand forward but, horrified,

saw that it still held the banana. Quickly switching it to his other hand, the Colonel passed the banana behind his back to the next person in line.

'Heard you'd moved here, Masters,' the General growled in his deep American drawl. 'Good. We'll be needing tight security on Project X.'

As the General went down the line, so the banana preceded him, passed with some embarrassment from one person to the next until it reached Mrs Janine White, Billy's mother and a scientist at the base. Next minute, Clarissa recovered her possession and stood in line.

'And this is Eldon, our Animal Psychologist,' Jameson introduced Jeff.

'I see they've given you an assistant,' laughed the General, nodding at Clarissa who was busy peeling the banana.

Everyone joined in the laughter as General Frank bent to shake hands with the chimpanzee, and Clarissa responded by throwing the banana skin over her shoulder where it landed before the centre's entrance doors.

The greetings over, General Frank moved towards the doors, but Colonel Masters threw out a sudden warning. 'Careful, sir.' He indicated the banana skin. 'Banana peel!'

'Glad you're here, Masters,' smiled the General,

taking care to step over the refuse. 'At this stage of the project we can't afford any slip ups, eh? Ha! Ha!'

Colonel Masters laughed at the joke and opened the door for the General to enter the building. Then, with glowering eyes, he swung round on Jeff. 'Now listen carefully, Eldon,' he snarled, stepping towards the open-mouthed Jeff. 'If I ever . . .!'

The remainder of Masters' sentence was lost to the skies as his heel landed firmly on the banana skin and he slid spectacularly off his feet.

The hilarious laughter which greeted Colonel Masters' unfortunate flight was in marked contrast to the sadness felt by a small boy just a few miles from the research base. Billy White stood at the door of his house, forlornly holding Digby on the new leash, while his grandfather pointed a wagging finger in the general direction of the countryside.

'Get him out, Billy,' thundered Mr White. 'OUT! O-U-T!'

Billy choked back the flood of tears that was about to gush down his cheeks. 'Can't he stay, Grandfather? Please?'

'Only when he learns to behave himself!'

Mr White slammed the door leaving Billy looking sadly down at the bundle of shaggy hair that shrouded Digby's face. 'Don't worry, Digby,' sobbed the boy. 'When mum comes home, she'll know what to do.'

It was as though Digby were crying too, for both boy and dog hung their heads in melancholy gestures and strolled slowly off down the road towards the research establishment.

What had started as a wonderful day for Billy was rapidly changing to one of the unhappiest he had known.

Chapter Two

THE THEFT OF PROJECT X

'Gentlemen, the success of Project X is vital to us all!' General Frank made the speech with a special edge to his booming voice. He was on his feet, addressing the principals of the research establishment in the long and impressive conference room. 'Not long ago,' he continued, 'the idea of growing fresh vegetables during prolonged space journeys seemed but an idle dream. Professor Ribart, I hear you've made strides.'

The professor coughed and stammered as he rose from his chair. His face beamed in boyish pleasure as he explained the details of his brilliant creation. 'Giant strides, General. We have actually grown a full sized cucumber from seed to maturity in exactly *twenty-six hours*.'

'Wunderbar!' interjected Doctor Harz, his eyes glazing as his thoughts took him into new times and dimensions. 'Staggering! Fresh peas on the way to Mars! Spring cabbage on Jupiter! Cauliflower on Capernicus!'

'There is a snag!' The hint of warning in Professor Ribart's voice commanded the full attention of the people at the conference.

'Snag?' questioned the General, his face grave. 'You can't eat them?'

'They're edible. Nutritionally perfect.'

'Then what is der snag?' Harz wanted to know.

Professor Ribart extended a hand to press a button on the table. 'I'll show you,' he said. The doors at one side of the room opened and Colonel Masters entered with a flourish before taking a smart jump to one side to allow another man to proceed into the room.

He wore a white, clinical-looking coat and resting on his shoulder was a large green object which, from a fairly sharp point, broadened out to a diameter of about four feet. He marched into the room, preceded by the ceremoniously erect Masters. The green object stretched out behind the white-coated assistant and through the door. As the seated men watched with mouths open, a second man appeared through the entrance, the green thing similarly supported on his shoulder.

Ten feet behind, a third man followed, then a fourth, and so on until the first man had gone out through the doors on the opposite side of the room. By the time the last man appeared with his ominous green load, the first had long since left the room.

General Frank gripped the edge of the table as Colonel Masters, with a snappy salute, closed the doors to shut out the incredible sight. 'That – that was the cucumber?'

'Yes, General,' nodded the Professor, his chest puffed with pride. 'The cucumber. We cannot stop it growing. Fascinating isn't it?'

'Fascinating!' snapped back the General. 'It's a tragedy. 'So—'

'So Project X is unusable,' announced Jameson, resignation in his voice, 'until we have found an antidote, something which will inhibit this uncontrolled growth. Of course we are working on it now. Mrs White has some interesting theories, but . . .'

Professor Ribart spread his hands in a helpless gesture. 'But until we find the antidote . . .'

'You have merely created a kind of vegetable Frankenstein's monster,' suggested Harz, and the conference ended.

Jameson returned to the relative quiet of his office and sat down at his desk. Outside he could hear the clatter of cups and saucers as the tea urn arrived in the corridor. 'I could do with a cup of tea,' he thought with some relief. Then the door opened and Jeff Eldon, annoyingly bright and cheerful, stepped in.

'Got a minute, sir?'

'No!' shouted Jameson grimly. Eldon was the last person he wanted to see.

'Oh, good,' smiled Jeff closing the door undeterred. 'Are you entering your roses in the Flower Show? I just had a great idea how we might grow a giant rose . . .'

Jameson's voice trembled with anger as the weight of his responsibilities crushed down on his mind. 'I do not want to discuss roses, Eldon! And on your way out tell Janine White I want to speak to her.'

Jeff accepted the situation and with a cheery wave he backed out of the office.

In the laboratory centre of the establishment, Janine White, Professor Ribart's assistant, and Billy White's mother, was enacting the daily ritual which Colonel Masters had insisted upon. Every morning he personally supervised the weighing of the entire stock of Project X.

As Janine added small brass weights to the delicate scales, Masters waited pencil poised ready to note down the exact measure of harmless-looking white powder contained in the glass jar.

'Four hundred and twenty-six grams . . . exactly,' Janine told him as the scales balanced.

'Four-two-six. Right,' agreed Masters, noting the amount down in his book. Then, with a fixed smile on his face, the Colonel moved to the laboratory's glass door. He hesitated for a second and then said, 'Doing anything for dinner tonight, Janine?'

'I'm sorry, Robert,' Janine answered with a nervous laugh. 'I promised to play monopoly with Billy after his homework.'

Suddenly the door flew open and smashed hard against Colonel Masters' nose.

'Janine . . .' called Jeff as he burst in. Then he saw Masters behind the door. He was looking dazed and had a handkerchief firmly clasped to his bleeding nose. 'Your nose is bleeding,' Jeff observed with some surprise. 'Best thing for it is a cold knife pressed against your upper lip.'

Jeff scooped up a surgical knife from a table. At once Masters adopted a karate stance.

'Watch it! I'm a black belt, you know!' Looking ridiculous, Masters edged around Jeff as if more disaster would strike. 'I'll see you later, Janine. Keep away from me you!'

'What was he doing behind the door?' Jeff asked when Masters had left.

'He was asking me to dinner.'

'From behind the door? No wonder you hit him on the nose!'

'I didn't,' laughed Janine. 'You did it with the door!'

'Hmm,' grunted Jeff seriously. 'He's pretty accident prone.'

Jeff moved into the room and stood close to Janine as she tried to resume her work. 'What are you working on?'

'I'm trying to find an antidote to that growth drug,' she answered as Jeff strolled up to a cage containing a pair of rabbits.

'It's not natural, Janine,' he said. 'You work far too hard. Look at these rabbits. They work here, too, but they do stop sometimes – at least they're human. And they're also very sociable. You never see a rabbit eating alone. They've got feelings. They eat together.'

Janine sighed deeply. She liked Jeff, but he was so awkward when it came to dealing with humans. 'Is this a roundabout way of inviting me to have dinner with your rabbits?'

'It doesn't really matter,' Jeff replied sombrely. 'I suppose you're having dinner with Colonel Nose Bleed anyway. A word of warning, Clarissa doesn't trust him.'

'Then she shouldn't go out with him,' Janine

laughed. 'Have you always loved animals, Jeff?'

Jeff thought for a moment. 'No, just my parents. Hold on, that doesn't sound right, does it?' He rummaged in his pocket and produced a photograph. 'What I mean is they were an animal act. On the stage.'

Janine looked at the picture of a comedy stage horse and suddenly understood.

'My mother was the head,' Jeff remembered, 'and my father was the – uh!' He returned the photograph to his pocket. 'They never split up. They were very happy together.'

'I'm glad,' smiled Janine, feeling great sympathy and friendship for this odd young man who was so kind. 'What was it you came to see me about?'

Jeff tried to remember. 'Oh, yes,' he said at last. 'Doctor Jameson wanted to see you right away. Sorry I forgot.'

Janine attempted to telephone Jameson, but Clarissa had taken over the switchboard, so the scientist decided to go to the doctor's office.

As the door closed, Jeff hesitated for a moment, then glancing about him, he adopted a rather furtive air. His eyes fell on the glass case in which the jar of white powder had been placed. Moving to the case, he slid up the glass front and stared at

Project X. Next moment he was withdrawing the jar and emptying a small quantity into an envelope.

'This isn't really stealing, Henry,' he said to the mouse who had been hiding in his pocket. 'But if it does that to a cucumber, what could it do for my roses?'

As Jeff sealed the envelope, Clarissa entered the room. Jeff replaced the jar carefully in the case and left the laboratory with his chimp.

Chapter Three

DIGBY DRINKS THE WRONG MILK

Billy White knew now what to do with Digby. Choking back the tears, he walked with slow steps in the wake of the shaggy-haired dog and turned into the gateway of a neat little cottage. Now the tears were falling, glistening down his cheeks as he tied Digby's leash to the front door of the cottage. A last sad glance at the tethered, whimpering dog, and Billy hurried away, his heart heavy with sorrow.

Minutes later, Jeff Eldon cycled down the lane and approached the same cottage. It was an ideal home for him. Just large enough for him to manage the household chores, and close to the research station.

Jeff saw Digby at once. With a broad grin he bent down to pat the dog's noble head.

'Hello, boy,' he said, and then noticed the note tied to Digby's collar. Printed in large capitals were the words:

DEAR MR ELDON. PLEASE TAKE GOOD CARE OF HIM. BILLY.

'Well,' Jeff said to the dog, 'You're a nice chap. I wonder what your name is? Never mind, we'll soon find you one. How about a drink?'

Jeff untied Digby and led him through into the small but tidy kitchen where he had most of his meals. He unclipped the dog's leash and then remembered the envelope containing the Project X powder. Filling a soup bowl with water, he stirred in the white powder until it took on the apearance of a milky liquid.

Just then, the back door bell rang. Jeff placed the bowl in the centre of the kitchen table out of Digby's reach, then hurried to the door. Janine White was there.

'I'm sorry about Digby,' Janine said at once.

'Digby?'

'The dog. That's his name. Father wouldn't have him in the house. I told Billy I thought you wouldn't mind looking after him for a bit. I hope you're not angry.'

Jeff pulled a funny face. 'Furious!' he said trying to sound annoyed. 'Digby and I were just going to have some milk. Will you join us?'

Janine sat herself at the kitchen table next to Digby who looked up from the floor with recognition all over his face. Jeff poured two glasses of milk, glanced about him, then making up his mind, pulled a chair across to a kitchen cabinet and climbed up to reach a number of tins stacked on the top.

'Why biscuits are always kept on the top shelf, I'll never know,' he said, trying to decide which of the tins contained anything other than air.

While Jeff struggled on, Janine noticed the bowl with the Project X liquid. Assuming it was milk, she placed it on the floor before Digby.

In a flash the thirsty dog had licked the bowl clean. By the time Jeff had found the biscuits and taken a chair at the table, Janine had refilled the bowl with milk, intending to give Digby another drink.

'No . . . No . . .' stammered Jeff, snatching it up. 'Er, I want him to get used to having his meals at regular times.'

Slightly puzzled, Janine took the biscuit Jeff offered her – an animal cracker – and sipped her milk.

'Janine,' Jeff then said, hesitating slightly. 'Did you know that the female of the species is not only more deadly than the male, but also untrustworthy, destructive and evil.'?

Janine smiled to herself, realizing that Jeff was

once more having difficulty in talking to a human being. 'Really,' she prompted.

'Yes. Take Sybil Apia for instance.'

'Who's she?'

'Sybil Apia's a queen bee,' Jeff explained. 'You know what a queen bee does? After her mate provides her with offspring she eats him. You really have to be very much in love with a girl to go through that!'

Janine stood up, gave Digby a pat and moved to the door. 'Jeff,' she smiled rather sadly as she made to leave. 'It's unlikely, I know. But if you ever do get around to asking me out to dinner, I promise I'll eat *it* not *you*! Bye Bye!'

Jeff stared at the closed door for a moment, shrugged his shoulders and then carefully carried the bowl out to the back garden. Stooping down, he slowly poured the liquid around the base of his prize rose bush. Satisfied, he stood back to survey his handiwork, then returned to the kitchen to give Digby a saucer of milk before starting work on another job that would make the dog feel more at home.

When animals were involved, Jeff found that he could be a real handyman with a set of woodworking tools. Soon he had completed the task of cutting a square hole in the back door, covering it with a hinged flap, and providing a simple exit for Digby.

'For your convenience, Digby,' Jeff laughed at the puzzled-looking dog. 'The freedom of the house, and garden.'

Digby was in no way sure what the flap was for, and he shied away from the opening as Jeff tried to push him through.

'There's nothing to be scared of,' Jeff insisted. 'Wait here. I'll show you.' Jeff went out of the door, closed it, and then dropped to his hands and knees opposite the flap. 'I know you've no mother or father to guide you, so look on me as father and do everything I do.' Jeff cleared his throat, and still on all fours started to imitate Digby's bark. 'Grrr! Woof! Woof!'

Meanwhile, in the next door garden, Doctor Harz, the establishment's psychiatrist, was being shown around the property by an estate agent.

'I'm sure you'll like the house, doctor,' the agent was saying, but Doctor Harz was not listening. He raised a quizzical eyebrow as he heard instead the growling dog noises drifting over the garden fence.

'Who lives next door?' Harz asked moving to the fence.

The agent, noticing Jeff, tried to bar Harz's way. 'A colleague of yours from the Research Centre. He's very quiet.'

Pushing the agent aside, Harz peered into the next garden. Jeff was continuing his demonstration of how to use the hatch. He barked and whined, scratched at the flap and wagged an imaginary tail. Then he let out a really loud bark.

Suddenly Jeff felt Harz's gaze upon him. He leapt to his feet, embarrassment causing a blush to spread over his cheeks. Smiling at the doctor, he gave a nervous wave and rapidly made for the safety of his kitchen.

Doctor Harz frowned with some concern, looked at the agent, but the man was beating a hasty retreat up the path. 'You signed the lease,' he said to the doctor with triumph in his voice, and Harz was left to scratch his head and wonder what exactly he had let himself in for in this strange neighbourhood.

Chapter Four

INTRODUCING TOM AND JERRY

Thomas and Gerald Wheeler, known to their circle of odd friends as Tom and Jerry, did not start out as crooks. There was a glorious moment in their lives when they were law abiding citizens of some fame. That was back in the days before they had the accident.

They had always been a little stupid, even at the height of their joint career as trapeze artists under the Big Top. In many ways that stupidity had led to their downfall. With regret they often remembered the day when Jerry had made a pile of sandwiches before taking to the bright lights to perform their high trapeze act. It was the butter which Jerry had forgotten to wipe from his hands that caused Tom to slither out of his brother's grasp at the crucial moment.

However, as one career ended, another began. Burglary was a far cry from the circus ring. The cheers of the crowd and the dazzling spotlight had been replaced by the quiet and darkness of nightly escapades into other people's homes.

Tom and Jerry were not good burglars. They tripped too many alarms and usually left the scene of their crime empty handed. But this night was something of an exception. True, they had alerted the police by clumsily sounding a burglar alarm, but they were showing a clean pair of heels to the law and in their hands was quite a haul of silver and valuables.

Escape was the prime consideration now. It would not be long before the pursuing policemen picked up their trail. They needed transport. Tom and Jerry ran down the line of cars parked in the driveway of the flats they had just robbed. Firm locks foiled them until, at last, a car door swung open offering them safe haven.

They did not realize the car was owned by the local police force, but even if they had known, they probably wouldn't have cared.

'Idiot!' A police sergeant yelled at the constable who ran from the flats to see the car roaring away. 'You forgot to lock the car.'

'They won't get far,' the constable smiled with confidence. 'I forgot to fill her up as well.'

As the two policemen broke into a run after the vehicle, Jerry urged Tom to drive faster. They managed to get as far as the next corner, but then the engine coughed and spluttered and the car crawled to a halt.

'We've run out of petrol,' Tom announced with surprise. 'Come on . . . let's make a run for it.'

The chase was on. Tom and Jerry took to the woods and found that they were still fit enough to remain ahead of the puffing, lumbering policemen. Then it seemed as if they were trapped.

A high wall confronted them, blocking off further escape.

'Quick!' hissed Tom. 'The old double-shoulder and back "S".'

Jerry instantly recognized the jargon. He stood with his back to the wall and waited for Tom to step back a few paces. Then with amazing agility, Tom ran and leapt up onto Jerry's shoulders and in a split second had reached the top of the wall.

Bending down, Tom gripped Jerry's outstretched hands and soon the brothers were together, clear of the policemen who could be heard bludgeoning their way through the trees. It was a fluid movement that brought Tom and Jerry down to the ground on the other side of the wall.

'We did it!' cheered Jerry, overjoyed. 'That's the first time we . . .'

'You want an encore?' snarled Tom sarcastically.

'You think we've got time?'

Tom gave Jerry a hard shove and they resumed the task of putting distance between themselves and the law. But the policemen were agile, too. Perhaps without the finesse of ex-circus performers, but certainly as effectively, the sergeant and his constable were soon taking up the chase once more, powerful flashlights blazing their paths. They had found a door in the wall. It was easy for them to walk through.

Vaulting a small fence, Tom and Jerry found themselves in a neat cottage garden. Keeping to the shadows they edged their way along until they reached the back door of the cottage.

A bright spot of light nearly picked them out, and it was all Tom could do to stop Jerry stepping out to perform in the nostalgic glow of bygone memory. Dropping to their knees, they crept beneath the range of the sweeping torch beam. That was how Tom found the flap cut in the foot of the door.

Tom crawled through and made Jerry jump with fright as he opened the door to allow his brother to enter. They glanced about them and were at once met by the steady, hair-shrouded gaze of Digby, squatting in the make-shift bed Jeff had prepared.

Digby let out a half-hearted bark. He was glad to have company, for since Jeff had gone to bed, he had felt lonely, and there was a strange sensation running around his tummy. Muffled voices and footsteps on the path outside told Tom and Jerry the policemen were not giving up the hunt.

'Hide!' Tom whispered fearing that the dog would alert the searchers.

Tom inched himself behind a heavy curtain leaving Jerry to dither in the centre of the sitting room. A large trunk stood against one wall and to Jerry that provided a hiding place. He opened the lid and holding the loot firmly in his grasp, disappeared inside it. Amused by Jerry's antics, Digby decided to put in a few words of approval at the entertainment. His bark woke Jeff who sleepily shuffled down the stairs from his bedroom.

'Digby,' the animal man grumbled, 'Go to sleep. There's no one here.'

Digby padded back to the trunk and Jeff returned to his warm bed, allowing Tom to emerge from behind the curtain.

'Stop playing with that dog,' Tom called in a hoarse whisper. 'Come on.'

Slowly the lid of the trunk opened and the head of a pantomime horse appeared. It took several seconds for Tom to realize that Jerry was wearing the head, but then he was making for the front door, and urging his brother to follow.

'Come on, the fuzz have gone.'

They hastily slid out of the front door, while Digby, sorry his new friends had left, barked sharply for them to come back.

That was the signal for Jeff to return to the ground floor. 'I told you to go to sleep,' he snapped, but Digby remained looking at the door and continued to bark. Jeff switched on the light.

Tom and Jerry had just enough time to push themselves flat against the wall each side of the entrance, so Jeff in his sleepy state did not notice them.

'See, dopey,' laughed Jeff. 'There's nobody there.' He bolted the door and led Digby back to the kitchen where the dog curled up in his bed. 'That's me for the night,' Jeff continued, bending low to bolt the flap. 'And you!'

Outside, Tom and Jerry heard the bolts rammed home.

'I just remembered something I forgot,' said Jerry in a faltering tone.

'What?'

'The silver!'

Tom let out a strangled cry and seized his brother.

'I left it in the trunk!'

'Congratulations. What did you want to do that for?' Tom snapped, his face red with rage.

'I had to, hadn't I?' stammered Jerry, looking like an innocent choir boy. 'If the law'd nicked us we'd have been clear wouldn't we?'

To attempt another break-in was out of the question. Instead, Tom gave Jerry a hefty slap across the shoulder and pushed him down the garden path.

Next morning, Jeff stretched and yawned himself awake, and slipping on a robe went down to greet Digby. At first he did not notice anything out of place. Then, slowly it dawned on him. 'Digby?' The word was tinged with disbelief. Jeff looked again at the dog. Yes, it was true. Digby had grown at least eighteen inches overnight. 'I never saw an animal grow so much in one night,' Jeff whispered, moving round the dog. 'Not even after Sybil ate her husbands.'

A thought sprang into Jeff's mind. Almost in panic he hurried outside and stared at the rose bush. It was exactly the same size as it had been on the previous day. Jeff glanced back through the open door at the huge dog. 'You didn't,' he said hoarsely. 'You couldn't, could you? You lapped up Project X!'

Chapter Five

DIGBY GROWS AND GROWS

Colonel Masters, Professor Ribart and Janine White glanced long and hard at the jar of Project X. There could be no doubt that the scales were correct. Masters bent closer to give the jar an extra special scrutiny.

'Sixty-eight grams definitely missing,' Janine said, reaching for the jar.

'Don't touch it!' Masters snapped.

Janine turned surprised eyes at him. He smiled knowingly and said, 'Fingerprints.'

'But who would want to steal ...?' began Janine as Masters took the jar by the neck with the aid of a handkerchief.

'Everybody,' answered Professor Ribart. 'Russians, Chinese, Americans.'

Jeff Eldon arrived in the laboratory at that precise moment. He saw the serious expressions on the faces of the other three and decided to stay in the background until he could get the chance to speak to Janine on her own.

'There's no sign of anyone breaking in,' Janine observed thoughtfully.

Masters sniffed grimly. 'There won't be. It's an inside job!'

'Someone here?'

'International Espionage,' nodded Masters pompously. 'Doctor Jameson must be told.'

With that Masters and Professor Ribart turned to leave. Masters saw Jeff and reacted quite violently. He gave the young man a very wide berth as if expecting trouble and, with a finger pressed against his lips, the Colonel motioned Professor Ribart to remain silent. Jeff's cheerful greeting was ignored and the two older men left the room.

Trying to appear disinterested, Jeff moved closer to Janine. 'Er – something wrong?' he asked.

'Someone stole sixty-eight grams of Project X powder during the night.'

'Who told you?' Jeff inquired – too quickly. 'Er – I mean how'd you know?'

'We weigh it every day. Since Colonel Masters took over security.'

Jeff gave the matter some thought and then seemed to decide this was a good opportunity to learn more about Project X.

'Janine . . . I was wondering, if an animal or a

human being ate some of this growth drug – would he go on growing, like the cucumber?'

'Well,' answered Janine, failing to notice the pointedness of Jeff's question, 'there's no absolute known limit to the size of vegetable life, but there does seem to be a limit to animal growth. There are big elephants, big men, but no giants or fairy-tale monsters as such.'

'That's a relief,' sighed Jeff.

'And, Jeff,' continued Janine, hardly noticing the sudden shock spreading over his features, 'don't worry about Digby too much.'

'Me, worry? Digby?' Jeff stammered.

'I think Father is changing his mind. I'll send Billy over for him.'

Jeff felt a wild panic grip him. 'OH!' he muttered in confusion.

'Is anything wrong?'

'Nothing,' replied Jeff holding his middle. 'My stomach. Something someone else ate . . . I mean . . . nothing.'

After work that morning, Jeff returned to his cottage to see how Digby was progressing. Progress was how Jeff now thought about the dog's growth, for as he went into the living room with a tin of dog food in his hand he could not disguise his shock.

Digby was the size of a small horse. Jeff glanced at the tin in his hand. 'Good news, Digby. You won't be growing *much* more.'

The dog gave a deep, thunderous bark that seemed to shake the cottage to its foundations.

'Hungry, eh,' Jeff gave a pathetic laugh as he showed the single tin to Digby, 'Well, this'll do for a start.'

Jeff moved into the kitchen to open the tin. He was about to scoop it into a soup dish when there was a knock on the back door. Jeff recognized the outline of Billy through the glass. Billy was whistling happily as Jeff cautiously opened the door.

'Mister Eldon,' the boy said, glancing at the dog food and the spoon held absentmindedly in Jeff's hands, 'I've come for Digby. Grandad says I can have him back again.'

Jeff hesitated then eased himself through the door and pulled it shut behind him. Now they both stood outside on the path. 'I'm afraid he isn't here,' Jeff lied. 'I – er – I gave him away.'

'Who to?' protested Billy in dismay.

'To a gypsy. Some old gypsy.'

'You shouldn't have done that,' Billy said without emotion. He was not sure what sort of game Jeff was up to, but he was pretty certain that this usually kind man was not telling the truth.

'Well, he was a poor lonely gypsy who'd lost his caravan,' Jeff went on, trying to make his voice sound convincing. 'All he had in the world was one gold earring.'

'You never told my mother about the gypsy,' Billy said with suspicion.

'What do girls know about lonely old gypsies? I'm sorry. I'll buy you another dog.'

Billy shook his head. 'I don't want another. I want Digby.'

Jeff took a deep breath. This was more awkward than he had imagined. 'That won't be possible . . .'

Suddenly Billy noticed the tin of dog food Jeff was holding. 'I think you've still got him,' he said with certainty. 'What are you doing with that?'

'It's my lunch,' Jeff replied at once.

'It's dog food.'

'Yes, but see what it says,' he pointed at the label and read, "So good, even Dad can eat it." Well I eat it.'

Billy frowned. 'All right then. Eat it!'

Jeff stared at the open tin. He stared at the spoon. He was trapped. There was no choice but to do as he was told. He plunged the spoon into the thick brown paste and scooped out a sample.

Billy's eyes stared up at him. Slowly he put the dog meat in his mouth and began to chew. It did not taste too bad, but the thought of eating tinned dog food definitely reacted violently against Jeff's digestive juices. He put on a brave face and munched on as if he enjoyed the mouthful.

In the next garden, Doctor Harz happened to glance over the dividing fence. He couldn't be sure if what he saw was true, but he decided to continue watching for a while.

Meanwhile, Jeff had bravely taken another spoonful of the dog meat. Watched closely by Billy he tried to keep up the act.

'Delicious,' smiled Jeff with difficulty. 'Try some.'

Suddenly there was a loud bark from within the cottage.

'You *have* got Digby. I'm going to tell my mother about you.' Billy whirled around and sped off down the path.

'No!' Jeff shouted after him. 'Don't do that! How would you like a chimpanzee? – I'll throw in a cage.'

But there was no stopping Billy until suddenly Doctor Harz leaned over the fence and grabbed his arm.

'That man mit which you are just now talking,'

Harz said in his broken English. 'He iss eating somethings, no!'

'Yes,' said Billy, tears in his eyes.

'Please, vot iss it?'

'Dog food!' Billy answered in a matter of fact voice, then he ran off down the lane.

Jeff stood outside his back door deep in thought. He nodded to himself, making up his mind what to do next, and tried to go inside the cottage. The door was locked and Jeff did not have his keys. Watched closely by Harz, Jeff fell to his knees and crawled through the two-way flap. Doctor Harz pulled a face and he, too, nodded. He had made up his mind about something also.

Chapter Six

JEFF IN A FIX

'Hello, Aunt Ina?' Jeff was talking on the telephone to his rather scatterbrained, but very lovable relation who lived in an isolated cottage deep in the country. Aunt Ina loved television. The set was on day and night and as her voice came over the receiver, Jeff could hear the strains of bagpipes as a Scottish tattoo was being shown.

Typically, Aunt Ina excused herself for a moment to adjust the television set and Jeff hung on to await her return. Suddenly the television volume went up, almost drowning out Aunt Ina's words as she said, 'That's better, I couldn't hear it!'

Jeff smiled to himself and then told his Aunt the reason for his unexpected call. 'I'll be down to see you tomorrow . . . and I'm bringing a friend.'

Jeff glanced at Digby, who was filling the living room, surrounded by hundreds of tins of dog food. Jeff wanted somewhere to hide Digby until he could think what to do, and Aunt Ina's isolated cottage would be ideal.

Jeff put down the phone and smiled up at the huge dog. 'All fixed, Digby. When I think about the experiments these scientists might carry out on you – I don't want to think about it.'

It was time for Jeff to return to work for the afternoon. He waved a fond farewell to the massive Digby, who seemed to be growing bigger by the minute, and jumped on his bike to pedal up the lane to the research centre. He passed the grey car parked down the lane, but did not see two men inside. They had slithered down below the windscreen with good reason to remain hidden, for they were Tom and Jerry, returned to recover their ill gotten gains.

As soon as Jeff was out of sight they crept up to his cottage and were soon inside. Together they moved towards the living room, and together they came to a sudden stop. 'Mother!' exclaimed Tom, as he looked across at the huge shaggy beast that seemed to fill the room. With a strangled cry, Tom turned and scampered for the hatch exit. He flew out of the house, rapidly pursued by Jerry, but Digby was roaring and growling close behind. By the time Jerry had escaped he had lost the seat of his pants and half a trouser leg.

Running faster than they dreamed possible, Tom and Jerry raced back to the car.

'It's impossible,' puffed Jerry. 'There never was a dog that size.'

'There is,' panted Tom in reply. 'And we're coming back tonight.'

'Let's forget the silver,' pleaded Jerry.

'Okay, forget the silver and take the dog.'

Forgetting his fear, Jerry stopped dead in astonishment. 'Not me,' he decided firmly.

Tom continued running to the car. 'Jimmy Rogerson would pay a lot of money to have a dog like that in his circus,' he called back.

Jerry was in the car almost as fast as his brother. 'He would, wouldn't he?' he said, a sly smile spreading across his face. With a grating of gears the two schemers drove away.

That evening, Jeff arrived home with a special treat for Digby. His knees buckling under its weight, Jeff had managed to get a bone from the butcher that matched Digby's enormous size and appetite. 'Digby?' Jeff called, uncertain of what sort of reception to expect from the dog. 'Only me. Got a surprise for you.'

As the door opened, Digby saw the bone and leapt forward like an express train. Jeff was bowled

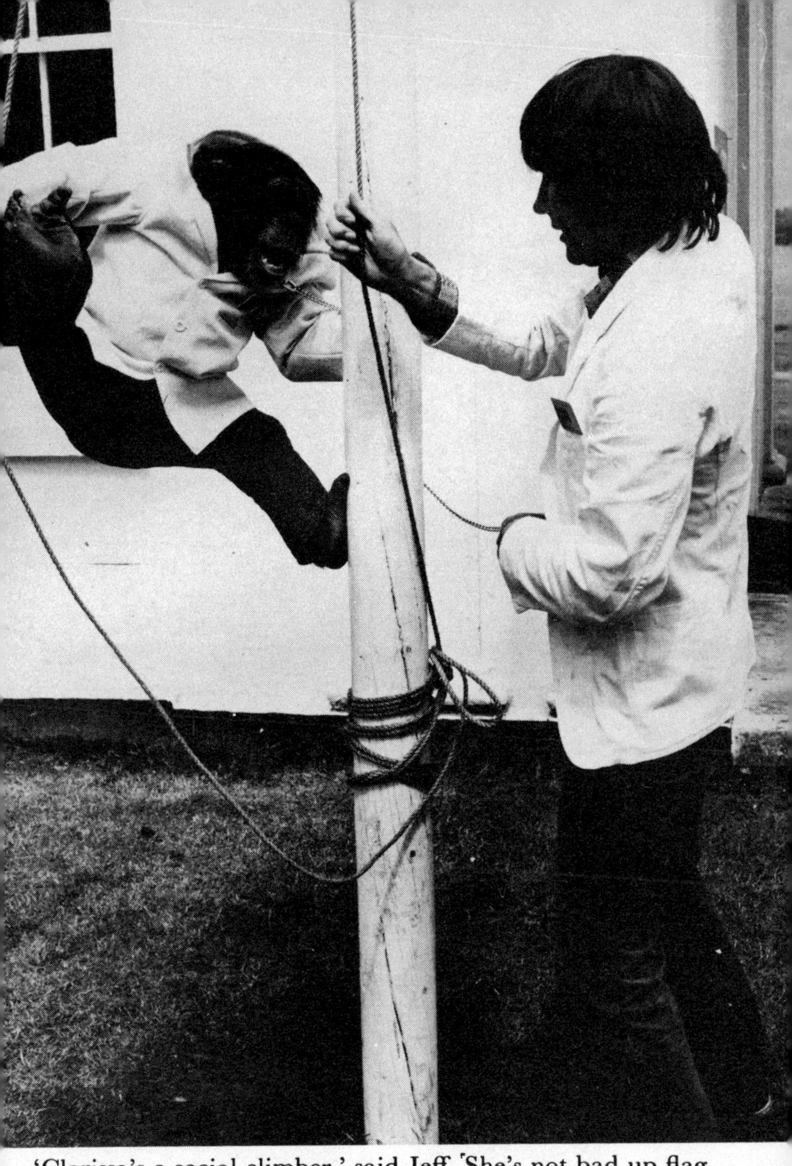

'Clarissa's a social climber,' said Jeff. 'She's not bad up flag poles, either'

The green object stretched out through the door, carried by the white-coated assistants

Clarissa had taken over the switchboard

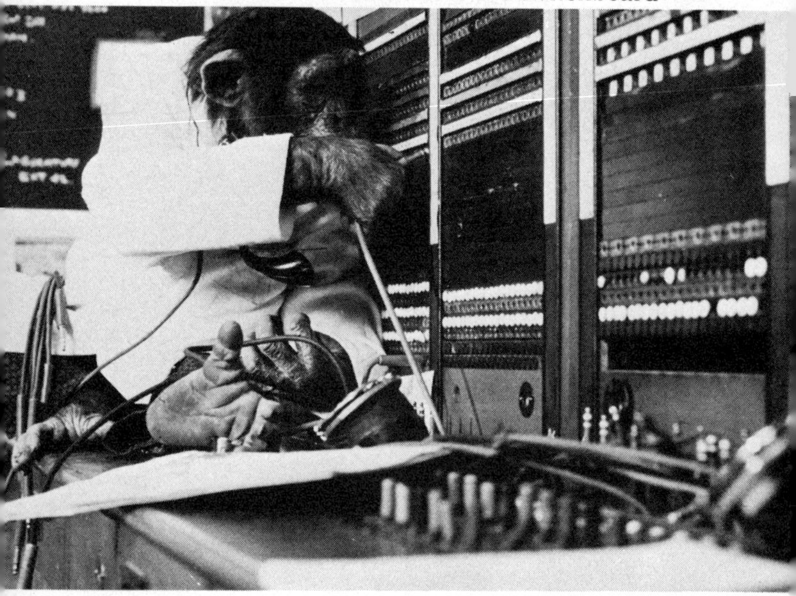

Jerry and Tom were not good burglars

Jeff took another spoonful of dog food. 'Delicious,' he said. 'Try some'

Jeff arrived home with a special treat for Digby

'You will be a good boy, won't you?' said Doctor Harz

When the board stopped, a blade had pierced Jeff's hat

At last, they heard Digby's unmistakable bark

Jeff and Billy gazed down to see the huge shape of Digby

Billy crawled into Digby's mouth to give him the antidote

aside by the tail-wagging boisterous mountain and the huge bone was snatched from his hand. It was several minutes before Jeff recovered sufficiently to go in pursuit of Digby. When he found the monster animal he screamed in alarm.

Digby had leapt the fence into Doctor Harz's garden and was furiously digging a hole in which to bury the bone. Already the hole in the middle of the doctor's lawn was fifteen feet deep. Jeff simply had to get Digby back into the house before anyone spotted him.

The bone had been discarded for a moment while the dog gave his impression of a mechanical steam shovel, so Jeff scooped it up and staggered back to his own cottage. Poised at the open door, Jeff shouted for Digby and in seconds realizing his prized possession had gone, the dog thundered towards the cottage.

At the last minute, Jeff hurled the bone into the house, waited for Digby to follow it, and then slammed the door shut. Without pausing, he grabbed a shovel from the garage and hurried next door to attempt to cover up Digby's tracks.

Doctor Harz chose that moment to arrive at his home with some furniture delivery men. At first he did not see Jeff, for a large wardrobe obscured the young man's frantic spadework from view. Then, as the men moved into the house, all was revealed.

'Mr Eldon,' said Harz gently, strolling towards the gaping chasm.

'Why the hole in mine garden you are making?'

'Uh?' stammered Jeff, gazing up at the eccentric German. 'It wasn't me.'

Doctor Harz climbed down to where Jeff stood speechless. 'You must see a doctor, my friend. Perhaps I see you? You are an interesting case.'

Slipping on the uneven earth, Jeff found himself lying on his back at the bottom of the hole. Doctor Harz did not hesitate. He joined the young man and stretched out beside him.

'I'm not a case,' protested Jeff. 'Please stop analysing me.'

'We will find out whether in your childhood,' Harz rambled on, ignoring Jeff's attempts to reassure the doctor of his sanity, 'you are loving a dog so much there comes a simple case of transference. You become a dog. So, you come to my office and lie on my nice *clean* couch.'

Harz stopped and glanced quizzically at Jeff. 'You will be a good dog won't you? You are housebroken, yes?'

Darkness had fallen over the research establishment, and there was just one flickering light coming from the office of Doctor Jameson. The light was caused by the beam of a slide projector as Colonel Masters demonstrated to Jameson the results of the fingerprint investigation made on the Project X jar.

'The glass had three definite sets of prints,' Masters said with an expert ring in his voice. 'Miss White's, which was to be expected.' He changed the slide. 'Eldon's – which was not . . .'

'Eldon's?' questioned Jameson in surprise.

'Yes,' answered Masters, changing the slide again. 'And a third set which is very mysterious indeed.'

'In what way?'

'They aren't human.'

'What the devil are you trying to say?' snapped Jameson.

'Well,' replied the Colonel, 'it's only an educated guess at the moment, but I *think* we'll find they are those of a *chimpanzee*.'

Jameson got to his feet in amazement. 'You're telling me that the spy is a chimpanzee?'

'Chimpanzees have a high I.Q.,' agreed Masters in a superior tone. 'They can be trained.'

'For goodness' sake, man,' shouted the doctor exasperated.

'Who threw the banana skin?' persisted the Colonel.

'The chimp,' nodded the research director. 'But that was an accident.'

'Was it? Let me ask you something else, sir. Who is in charge of the animal?'

'Eldon?'

'Exactly, Eldon!' nodded Masters in triumph.

'But he was screened like everybody else,' protested Jameson.

Colonel Masters bounced on his heels with supreme confidence. 'Every spy that got in anywhere has been screened like everybody else. Incidentally, I think our computer needs overhauling.'

'Why?'

'I decided to check Eldon's record,' answered the security man. 'The answer card came out saying his parents were a horse!'

'You pressed the wrong button,' argued Doctor Jameson.

'I did it twice.'

There was a sharp rap at the door, and Doctor Harz marched in with a worried expression on his face. 'Excuse, please,' he snapped. 'I must speak with you about someone who has the very serious problem.'

'Who?' asked Jameson.

'Mister Jeffery Eldon.'

Jameson and Masters exchanged glances and suddenly became more interested in what Doctor Harz had to say. 'What about Eldon?'

'He thinks he's an animal,' replied Harz sitting in Jameson's vacant chair.

'A horse?' Masters and Jameson asked together.

'What horse?' scoffed Harz. 'Nein – a dog! He thinks he is a dog.'

'Our computer says his parents are a horse, but *he* thinks he's a dog.' Doctor Jameson could hardly believe his own words. He was supposed to be a responsible adult, and yet here he was discussing whether or not a colleague was an animal. 'Why should anyone in his right mind think he's a dog?'

'Exactlich!' exclaimed Harz. 'He is not in his right mind. Gentlemen, what we are witnessing is a return to an expression of antagonism against society and the world. One area of his brain has regressed to earliest primitive man when they talked with barks and grunts.'

Jameson gave the matter some thought for a few seconds. 'Perhaps I'd better go round and talk to him,' he decided at last.

'Perhaps mit the ambulances and straight jackets,' agreed Harz. 'And maybe a leash!'

Masters adjusted his cap. 'I'll come too, sir. Just in case. You might need protection.'

Jameson headed for the office door and then another thought struck him. 'Um, Harz,' he said softly. 'When we meet Eldon should we speak or – well – bark at him?'

Harz stood up, paced the room, then made up his mind. 'Simply *spik*!' he told them with determination. 'Bark and you never know what you are saying to a dog!'

Chapter Seven

DIGBY IS STOLEN

It was close to midnight. Slowly the cottage door opened and Jeff glanced to left and right, checking that the coast was clear. Satisfied that there were no unwelcome witnesses, the young animal man opened the door wider to allow Digby to pass through into the garden.

Jeff paused on the way to the gate to examine the creature he was leading. The feet were big and fluffy with shaggy hair brushing the path, but the head and body were a strange sight and closer in appearance to a horse than a dog. In order to disguise Digby's unheard of size, Jeff had put the pantomime horse costume over the dog.

'Digby,' he said, a lump in his throat. 'I could cry. You look just like Mum and Dad.'

Digby gave a throaty bark, muffled by the costume's head, and Jeff moved with faster steps to get the dog safely into the horse box he had rented. Before Jeff could drive away, another car came quietly down the lane. Inside were Tom and Jerry. They had come to snatch Digby from the cottage.

'The crafty devil,' muttered Tom as he heard Digby bark from within the trailer. 'He's ripping off with the dog.'

'Then we've lost him, 'aven't we?' observed Jerry with some relief. He was still remembering the half trouser leg he had lost earlier that day.

But Tom was not to be so easily discouraged. 'You are about to take part in the first horsebox hi-jacking,' he breathed with excitement, and as Jeff's tail lights moved on down the lane, Tom crashed the gears of his car to follow.

Through the night the two cars drove, Jeff heading north towards his aunt's remote house; Tom and Jerry never far behind. Soon after dawn, near Newmarket, Jeff pulled into a roadside café and settled down to enjoy a hearty breakfast. This was Tom's and Jerry's chance, they decided as their car, with its empty trailer, stopped beside the café.

'Let's see how friendly the dog is for a start,' suggested Tom as he crossed to a trailer, not realizing that it wasn't Jeff's.

'Got any sugar?' Jerry asked seriously.

'He's a dog not a horse, stupid,' Tom snapped. 'Go on, have a look. I'll keep watch.'

Jerry watched his brother saunter round to the

front of the café where he could see Jeff through the window. Shrugging his shoulders, Jerry unhooked the trailer's tailgate and lowered it to the ground. Next second he was flying through the air with the shrill whinny of an irate stallion echoing in his ears.

Tom hurried back and took in the situation at once as he saw the rear view of the horse in the box. 'Try that one,' he told Jerry as he rose groggily to his feet.

Jerry hesitated while Tom replaced the tailgate.

'Go on,' urged Tom chirpily. 'I'll keep watch.'

Ducking below the window of the café, Tom and Jerry reached Jeff's trailer and peered into the gloomy interior. At once Digby nosed his head to confront them.

'Crafty,' chuckled Tom. 'He's put the dog in the horse. Let's get him into our . . .' A sudden idea struck Tom. He savoured the thought for an instant and then turned to his brother. 'I've got a better idea. You unhook the trailer with the horse in it and hook it on to Eldon's car. Go on, I'll keep watch.'

Unaware of Jerry's strenuous exertions, Jeff continued to tuck into his eggs and bacon, watched carefully by Tom. Then the first part of the switch was completed.

'Now,' instructed Tom, 'you take Eldon's trailer

with the dog in it and you hook it onto our car. Go on, I'll keep watch.'

Once again, the sweat pouring down his face, Jerry set to work to haul the trailer around the café. Near to collapse, he staggered back to Tom.

'Right,' Tom said with a determined nod. 'Now you take our trailer with nothing in it and hook it onto the car that had the horse. I'll keep watch.'

Finally, as Jeff left the café, the complicated manoeuvring was completed and with great relief Jerry slumped into the passenger seat of their car, while Tom watched both Jeff and the owner of the other car drive off.

With a satisfied nod, Tom let in the clutch and pulled away, only to realize that Jerry had failed in at least one respect. He had failed to hook Digby's trailer to the car. A quick reverse, a smashing of his rear lights and the matter was put to rights. Then Tom and Jerry were off with their prize . . . the biggest dog in the world.

Chapter Eight

DIGBY JOINS THE CIRCUS

It took Jeff Eldon several minutes to convince his Aunt Ina that he was not the milkman, or postman, or the gasman. But Jeff took it in good humour, for his aunt was always thinking about other things; never concentrating on reality. That's why the television set played such a big part in her life.

At the fourth attempt Jeff managed to gain entry into the cottage where he explained that the 'friend' he had brought was a dog the size of a horse. Aunt Ina did not find anything Jeff told her at all strange. To her a horse-sized dog was just another incident that made up life's rich pattern.

'Let's have a look at this monster,' Aunt Ina suggested, commenting on the length of Jeff's hair.

Standing behind the trailer, Jeff did not bother to look in, he was more interested in the reaction on his aunt's face. 'Aunt Ina, meet Digby,' he introduced.

'I thought you said he was a dog,' Ina said staring into the eyes of the switched race horse. 'It's a horse.'

'No,' corrected Jeff with a smile. 'That's Mum and Dad's old stage costume. Digby's a . . .' Jeff for the first time looked up to where the race horse had thrust its head over the trailer's tailgate . . . a horse! His eyes popped. 'But I left home with a dog!'

'That turned into a horse,' agreed Aunt Ina, humouring her nephew.

'Yes . . . No!' stammered the animal man in confusion. 'Wait . . . Digby must have been switched . . . when I turned in to a café.'

'You turned into a café?' laughed Aunt Ina, glad that her visitor was providing her with such fun.

Many miles from Aunt Ina's cottage, two men were not finding their present task in the least bit amusing. Tom and Jerry were straining every muscle to carry a huge tin bath towards a derelict garage. Inside the bath were piles of meat and other titbits designed to satisfy the ravenous hunger of their new guest, Digby.

The Wheeler Brothers opened the garage doors expecting to see a large dog the size of a horse. They were greeted by an incredibly loud growl and a bark that nearly shattered their ear drums. There was a large dog in the garage, but now Digby's head was touching the ceiling. He was fully fifteen feet high.

With screams of fear, Tom and Jerry hastily slammed shut the garage doors preventing their monstrous investment from escape.

'He's growing every minute,' mumbled Tom, wiping his brow. 'The sooner we see Jimmy Rogerson the better.'

At Aunt Ina's cottage the television was on. Jeff was enjoying a quiet cup of tea and a biscuit when he took a sudden interest in a news item that came from an announcer.

'. . . the racehorse was being transported to Cheltenham. Police would like to interview Mr Jeffery Eldon, an animal psychologist at the NATO Research Centre, who may be able to help them in their enquiries, regarding the theft of a missing secret project. When last seen, Mr Eldon was driving a car with a horse box in tow . . .'

Jeff jumped to his feet with a start. 'Which he is now going to get rid of!' he said with certainty as he hurried out to the barn where the horse was stabled.

Rogerson's circus was a small, travelling outfit that

toured the country with a handful of star turns. The circus did not make a lot of money, but the circus tradition was in Jimmy Rogerson's blood and his performers were not really good enough to get work elsewhere.

Tom and Jerry arrived at the circus ground to be greeted with cheery shouts from the artistes' children, for despite their new and unsavoury profession, the Wheeler Brothers were remembered with affection. They made their way past the Big Top to a large and splendid caravan that was the home and office of their one-time boss. Charlie, a ferret faced midget opened the door to their knock, and the greeting he gave them was far from friendly.

'Is the boss in?' Tom asked, wary of Jerry's reaction to the little man. There was no love lost between his brother and Rogerson's right hand man.

Reluctantly Charlie admitted Tom and Jerry into the confines of the trailer where the tall and moustached Jimmy Rogerson was in no mood to see the act that had once all but ruined his business.

'Well, well,' grunted the big man sarcastically. 'Look who's here . . . the Brothers Death!'

Tom ignored the scathing remark and chirpily announced his scheme. 'Jimmy, have we got something for you!'

'You'll make a fortune,' added Jerry with enthusiasm.

'I can't afford it,' countered Rogerson flatly. 'Show them out, Charlie.'

'Wait,' Tom hurried on. 'We've got something that'll bring the public in by the thousands – and all we ask is fifty percent.'

'Of what?' asked Rogerson still disinterested.

Tom drew in his breath and allowed a hushed atmosphere to descend on the trailer. When he spoke again, his words were slow and deliberate. 'The biggest dog in the world!'

The mood Tom had tried to create was lost on the big man. 'Dogs!' Jimmy grunted, putting out a hand to measure the height of his midget companion. 'I'm up to here in dogs!'

'Jimmy,' Tom continued quickly. 'Why stand arguing? The dog's here. What's it cost to take a look?'

Exchanging glances, Jimmy and Charlie had a silent consultation before both men agreed with nods of their heads, and they followed Tom and Jerry out of the trailer to the car park.

A large furniture van stood before them, and with a theatrical air, Tom and Jerry slowly opened the large top doors. Jimmy Rogerson stared up at the opened van. There, with his head scraping the roof, was Digby, huge, shaggy, brown eyes gazing down at the speechless circus man.

Digby opened his mouth, gave one thunderous bark and Jimmy Rogerson fell backwards like an axed tree trunk. The shock had been so severe he had fainted on the spot.

'And I thought he liked animals,' chuckled Tom, knowing full well that their prize act had impressed the hard-bitten circus owner. Tom and Jerry would be in business . . . as soon as Rogerson recovered his senses.

Since Jeff Eldon had tried to fool Billy White into believing that Digby had been given away, the boy had not shown interest in much at all. He moped about his home, getting under his grandfather's feet, and generally remained disillusioned with the whole world. Without enthusiasm he was at the moment watching television, his mind on the great tragedy that had come into his life. On the screen, a sneering, disbelieving programme reporter was saying something about a circus and the fact that some disturbance was being created by the introduction of a new act.

'They are trying to tell us that the dog is as big as a house,' chuckled the man, a forced smile on his lips. 'Yes, folks, we are told that this mammoth hound will go on show to the public this afternoon in the Big Top . . .'

A poster showing Tom, Jerry and Jimmy Rogerson standing before the towering image of Digby was flashed on the screen.

'His name is King . . .' continued the announcer with a derisive chuckle.

Billy sat up and took notice. Something about the massive dog struck a chord of recognition in his mind.

'It's Digby!' Billy said forcefully.

Mr White sat close by reading his newspaper. Billy tugged at his grandfather's sleeve. 'Grandad,' he yelled in excitement. 'That's Digby.'

The old man peered over his glasses at the poster on the screen. 'No,' he shook his head. 'It's just one of their tricks.'

The television personality continued to poke fun at the thought of a twenty-five feet high dog. 'We were assured that the circus would be happy to allow King to be presented to you,' he laughed, his lip curling. 'But unfortunately he's too big to get into the studio!'

The man was enjoying himself beyond all measure, but to Billy it was not a joke. He was convinced. 'It *is* Digby!' he shouted, and ran out of the house.

At the same time, many miles away in the north of England, Jeff Eldon and Aunt Ina were also watching a television screen. Jeff, too, saw the poster advertising King, the biggest dog in the world. 'It's Digby!' Jeff shouted in amazement as he leapt to his feet. 'Goodbye, Aunty. I've got to go!'

Chapter Nine

DIGBY IS A SENSATION

The television programme announcing Digby's – alias King's – arrival at the circus certainly captured the imagination of the public. In their thousands the intrigued spectators flocked to Rogerson's Big Top to discover whether there was such a huge animal.

'Ladies and Gentlemen,' Jimmy Rogerson shouted through a loud hailer as he stood at the entrance to the massive tent. 'We are absolutely full. Sorry, there's no room left. Tickets for tomorrow's performance are now being sold at the Box Office.'

On the edge of the disappointed crowd, Jeff Eldon pulled a face and moved away, wandering around the side of the Big Top towards the other tents and caravans scattered about the site.

At the front of the crowd, below Jimmy Rogerson's long legs, Billy White was not to be put off quite so easily as the circus owner bellowed once more, 'Sorry ladies and gentlemen, there are no seats left for today's performance. Today's performance is absolutely sold out!'

With great pride and satisfaction, Tom and Jerry, immediately behind Rogerson, were mentally counting their share of the entrance money. They did not notice Billy as he crept past them and managed to duck under the canvas and into the Big Top. A friendly ice cream salesman found him a seat, for someone as small as Billy could squeeze in anywhere.

Jeff was not having such good fortune. Strolling around the outside of the big tent, he could find no way in. But then he noticed an adjacent tent that appeared to be empty. He realized that it was the dressing room area, and was soon sitting down before a mirror absentmindedly playing with the false noses, funny wigs and clown's hats.

Making up his mind, he began to apply some clown make-up and, pleased with the result, realized that this could be his ticket into the arena.

'Hurry up, mate,' said a jovial clown as he hurried past heading for the tented corridor that led to the circus ring itself. 'You'll be late for the parade.'

So far so good. Jeff had managed to fool one of

the circus regulars. He stood a good chance of getting away with his disguise.

The circus band struck up a fanfare and brassily continued into the opening parade march, and as the clowns delighted the huge audience Jeff put the finishing touch to his costume, a tall black hat. The Ringmaster took up the microphone and made the first announcement. 'And now, for your added pleasure and entertainment, ladies and gentlemen – the Great Manzini!'

The Great Manzini was the main part of a knife throwing act. Unfortunately, he was nearly blind and the ridiculous pebble-glassed spectacles he wore hardly helped. A revolving board was wheeled into the ring and a pretty assistant looked around for the Great Manzini's target.

Jeff by this time had edged his way into the Big Top and, to his surprise, the girl caught his hand and led him to the board. If Jeff, in the beginning, did not know why he was leaning against the apparatus, he was soon to find out as a sharp bladed knife flashed through the air to pin his trailing sash belt to the board. Unable to move, Jeff was forced to stand there, protesting vigorously as one by one the knives thudded around him.

And now the Great Manzini was haltingly led to the edge of the ring. Blindfolds were put round his eyes and a thunderous drum roll pealed through the Big Top as he started to run towards Jeff to throw the final knife. Jeff uttered a fearful scream as he felt the girl rotate the board he was pinned to. The Great Manzini tripped, the knife left his hand, and Jeff heard it thud into the board. When the board was brought to a standstill, the crowd cheered as they saw that the blade had pierced Jeff's tall hat, missing the top of his head by a fraction.

After the great ovation, no one in authority took any notice of Jeff's presence at the side of the arena. They were too busy preparing for the next act.

The Ringmaster took up his position in the centre and shouted, 'And now, ladies and gentlemen, the moment which you have all been waiting – for! The most staggering sight to be witnessed by man since dinosaurs ruled the world.'

Jimmy Rogerson, Tom and Jerry made their way to an acrobat's see-saw to wait the applause.

'A creature so large,' continued the Ringmaster, 'that it defies description. Jimmy Rogerson in conjunction with fellow impressarios Thomas and Gerald Wheeler proudly present *King! The Biggest Dog in the World!*'

All eyes turned to the Big Top entrance. A hush

descended on the huge crowd. Then, as the shimmering silk curtains opened, the awesome sight of Digby appeared. The trumpets were sounding a thrilling fanfare, circus performers on stilts, acrobats, and a complete cavalcade of colour and movement revolved around the magnificent figure of the shaggy haired dog.

A tractor began to chug slowly forward, hauling Digby into the centre of the ring, and Billy White gasped as he saw that his pet was chained to a wheeled platform.

The crowd murmured in disbelief and amazement. They could not believe their eyes.

'Yes, ladies and gentlemen,' shouted the Ringmaster again. 'You are not imagining it. Impossible you say, but nevertheless – true! *King*!'

Billy suddenly rose to his feet. 'No!' he roared. 'It's Digby! DIGBY!'

The monstrous dog heard the assured cry from Billy. He turned his head in the direction of his old friend and master and opened his mouth to utter an earth-shaking bark. The noise was so deafening, the audience started to scream and panic. Some high-wire acrobats took fright and leapt to the ground, landing on the higher end of the see-saw. Tom and Jerry had the smiles wiped off their faces as they were shot, in the same movement, straight up into the air to land on the bars of the swinging trapeze.

Billy White, excited at seeing his pet once again, ran down to the ring calling, 'Digby! Here Digby!'

The magnificent beast tugged at the chains which secured his feet. One by one they snapped and, with the crowd streaming in all directions in blind terror, Digby became alarmed and started to lumber out of the Big Top. No one tried to stop him. There was little anyone could do. Digby was free and his massive strides took him rapidly from the circus field and out into the country.

Left behind was a scene of great confusion. People ran in all directions, while high above them Tom and Jerry involuntarily swung on the trapeze, hurtling back and forth through the air. Jerry decided he was too scared to continue with this death-defying accidental show, and he released his hold on the bar and grabbed Tom round the waist. Slowly, Tom's trousers slid down his legs and the two brothers fell earthwards, to land crushingly on the irate Jimmy Rogerson.

Billy had seen Digby's exit from the Big Top and he tried in vain to follow, pushing through the milling crowds until he was brought to a standstill by the weight of numbers. Then a funny-looking clown was at his side, offering an outstretched hand.

'Here, Billy, this way,' said a familiar voice, but Billy could not place the man's grotesque features.

Jeff snatched off his false nose and the clown's wig. 'It's me, Billy – Jeff Eldon.' Billy breathed with relief, forgetting the anger he felt for the man whom he believed had betrayed him, and together they ran out of the tent.

'Come on,' said Jeff, still holding Billy's hand. 'Digby went this way.'

Chapter Ten

DIGBY ON THE RUN

Digby's escape from the circus was a prelude to a wave of emotional and sometimes inaccurate reports from places throughout the West Country. The dog's monstrous size caused him to be clumsy where houses and trees were concerned and Digby's proportions automatically threw people into alarm and confusion.

The NATO Research Establishment was soon the scene for an emergency meeting. Doctor Jameson, Professor Ribart, Janine White and Colonel Masters had a more than passing interest in Digby's activities, for they coupled the disappearances of Project X and Jeff Eldon with the dog's rapid growth.

'It's incredible!' grunted Doctor Jameson in a tone approaching hysteria. 'And if that dog continues to grow like that cucumber – the dog must be found and destroyed.'

'Don't forget Eldon,' put in Colonel Masters. He

had not found it difficult to build up quite a hate campaign against the animal man.

'We don't want to destroy Eldon, do we?' Jameson asked in amazement.

There was a wicked gleam in the eyes of the security man, but he let it pass. 'I wonder who is paying him for this?'

Janine White was staggered. Unlike the Colonel, she remained loyal to Jeff. 'Paying him?' she asked.

'You said he enquired about the drug's possible effect on animals,' explained Masters. 'Janine, imagine three-hundred million Russians all fifty feet tall...'

'That's how I always imagined them,' put in Jameson drily. Then he began the business of organizing a full scale search for the missing Jeff, Billy and Digby.

Billy stretched his arms and felt the warm, early morning sun on his face. He got to his feet and looked about him trying to remember where he was. Jeff Eldon's sleeping form brought back the events of the previous day. They had chased after Digby, moving deep into the country, but then darkness and exhaustion had overtaken them and the haystack Billy now found himself resting against had provided a warm bed for the night.

Then Billy remembered something else. He did not count Jeff Eldon amongst his friends. This was all his fault . . . Digby, everything was the doing of Jeff, Billy felt sure.

Billy went to creep away, but Jeff was awake by now. 'Billy, where are you going?'

'To look for Digby,' replied the boy sullenly.

'Alone? Without me?'

Billy paused for a moment as Jeff came up to him.

'I don't trust you,' he said softly. 'You lied to me about giving him away to some lonely gypsy. And it wasn't true.'

'I'm sorry,' Jeff answered, sitting down on the hay and motioning for Billy to do the same. 'I didn't want you to know what had happened to him, that's all.'

'What happened?' asked the boy.

'He kept growing and growing and the more he grew, the more I couldn't tell you.'

'Why did he keep growing?'

Jeff sighed deeply. This was going to be the hard part. 'You wouldn't understand it,' he said at last. 'It's too scientific.'

'I understand one thing,' Billy murmured sadly. 'You're not my friend and you're not Digby's friend.'

Jeff was shocked by the boy's words. He gazed deep into Billy's tearful eyes and said with feeling, 'I'm everyone's friend . . . especially animals. The first person I ever loved was a dog. I was your age . . . and my dog was the cleverest in the neighbourhood. I used to throw a stick and say "fetch".'

'What's so clever about that?' Billy wanted to know.

'He just lay down and let me do the fetching.' Jeff paused to watch the slim smile touch at the corners of Billy's mouth. 'He was a Basset Hound,' the young man continued while he had Billy's attention. 'He had the saddest face. His name was Happy. He was a great watchdog. If a robber ever broke into the house he would sit there and watch.'

Jeff adopted the expression of a sad-faced Basset Hound, dropping his jaw and pulling in his cheeks in a miserable grimace. Again the smile, broader this time, came to Billy's lips. 'And he looked so sad, no one would ever steal anything. They would just cry a little and leave.'

Billy laughed aloud and Jeff jumped to his feet. 'C'mon, Billy,' he smiled. 'Let's find Digby – together.'

Holding hands, the two moved off across the fields. Billy felt better. Jeff was really a kind man, he decided. Perhaps it was not his fault that Digby had landed up in such trouble.

For the chiefs and directors of NATO, and in particular the Research Centre that developed Project X, a crisis point had been reached. A high-level conference was arranged at which government and military heads allowed General Frank to preside.

'I don't want to step on anybody's toes,' the General began cautiously, aware of the medals and gold braid that stared back at him from the table. 'But . . .'

Suddenly the door burst open and in marched Colonel Masters, as pompous as ever, his chest stuck out like a cockerel's. 'I've got it, sir,' he announced in triumph.

'What?' Doctor Jameson asked flatly.

'The Russians' new heavy-duty helicopter,' answered the Colonel, pleased with the astounded looks he had managed to bring to the faces of his superiors. 'Tremendous lifting power. They've offered us the use of it. Relax, I'm on top of the problem.'

With that, Colonel Masters gave a sharp salute and marched out of the room leaving the generals and admirals open-mouthed.

Unfortunately, the helicopter proved as unsuccessful to trap Digby as the chains which Jimmy Rogerson had imagined would contain the huge animal. Tempted by a vast quantity of meat, Digby was drawn into a waiting net, but as the helicopter rose to lift the giant dog, Digby decided to struggle and run.

The result was a grounded Russian aircraft and a very red-faced Colonel Masters who had directed the whole disastrous operation.

Further incidents of Digby's rampage across the country flooded into the news services and when a passenger train driver had a narrow escape sending his train directly under the mammoth dog who had decided to rest on the railway tracks, official opinion hardened and all agreed that drastic action should be taken at once.

A second top-level conference was convened at the Research Centre and Doctor Jameson made a grave announcement. 'The Russians,' he said with a slight twitch at the corner of his mouth, 'are sueing us for a new helicopter.'

General Frank had reached the end of his patience. He jumped to his feet and in a loud voice declared, 'I am alerting two full military units. Gentlemen, the order now is –' he waited for the gathering to turn their florid faces towards him. 'Seek and destroy!'

The momentous decision had been made, but for Digby, water was the main priority as he continued to pace his giant way across the countryside. He found the water, a largish pool, and drained it dry.

Hard on Digby's heels came Jeff and Billy, relentlessly pursuing their favourite animal friend. They found the dried up lake and knew their quest would soon be at an end.

Long hard miles lay ahead of them before, at last, they heard Digby's unmistakable bark. The sound came from a steep-banked quarry and when Jeff and Billy struggled to the crest of the ridge, they gazed down to see the huge, shaggy, wonderful shape of Digby, the biggest dog in the world.

'Quiet, boy!' Jeff said in a soothing voice as he helped Billy to reach the exhausted animal. 'Quiet, Digby.'

Billy was as tired as the dog. He looked up at the great shaggy mountain and tears welled into his eyes. 'We've got to do something quick,' he cried in despair. 'Why does everybody hate Digby? Why do they want to harm him?'

'Nobody really hates him,' Jeff answered, trying to comfort his young companion. 'They don't even know him. But they're scared, Billy. And scared people do funny things.'

'He doesn't mean any harm,' sobbed Billy, burying his face in his hands.

'No,' agreed Jeff, 'but to them he's a monster, simply because they've never seen a giant dog before.'

Jeff gripped Billy's shoulders and gazed directly into his fear-filled eyes. 'Billy, I'll do anything before I let them get Digby.'

Billy thought for a moment and shook his head. 'What can you do against the army?'

'We've got one last chance,' Jeff said, climbing to his feet. 'I'll need your help, Billy. Stay here with Digby. Don't move from this hiding place. I'll be back as soon as possible.'

Jeff climbed the high side of the quarry and waved back at Billy and Digby. Then he was lost from their view. Billy laid his head near his pet's paw and went to sleep.

Jeff reached a main road and went through the frustrating and tedious business of thumbing a lift. He was on his way back to the Research Centre, but it would be nightfall before he reached it.

Chapter Eleven

JEFF TO THE RESCUE

Janine White was checking her notes in the laboratory when Doctor Jameson came in.

'Janine, why don't you go home?' he said in a gentle, comforting voice. 'It's late and you're worn out.'

'I'd go crazy without doing something.' Janine started to prepare a small dictation machine, ready to record more data on her work.

'Try not to worry too much about Billy,' Jameson continued. 'He'll come to no harm, even if he is with Eldon.'

Janine thought about the situation. She had long since stopped crying for Billy. There didn't seem to be any tears left.

'Jeff went crazy, didn't he?' Mrs White muttered sadly. 'You heard what Doctor Harz said.'

'Harz!' Jameson scoffed as he moved to the door. 'I'm not too sure about him either. Don't stay too late. It's almost dawn. We'll get Billy back.'

Doctor Jameson left the Research Centre before Jeff's arrival. The young animal man had managed to travel through the day and was determined to help Digby, if it was at all possible. He hesitated at the gates of the establishment, for a uniformed guard and police dog stood as sentry, checking all visitors.

But Jeff had timed his approach to perfection. He knew the guard routine, and sure enough, as he watched, the civilian gate keeper in the small gate house tapped on the glass and beckoned the soldier.

'Tea up,' called the man, and the soldier looked down at the dog.

'Bruce! Sit! Guard!'

The Alsatian obediently did as he was told, while his handler hurried into the gatehouse for his usual cup of tea. Jeff waited a couple of minutes until he was sure the guard was settled, then he tiptoed towards the dog.

'Morning, Bruce,' Jeff winked at the animal who wagged his tail in return. Of course, being animal psychologist to the base gave Jeff a distinct advantage. Every animal was his friend.

In the laboratory, Janine was operating the tape recorder. '. . . the antidote's retroactive propensities,' she dictated, 'can therefore be said to exist. However, success cannot be claimed until we can be assured that the retroactive process can be controlled, since an uncontrollable process would result in the total destruction of the subject treated with the antidote . . .'

Janine suddenly stopped, aware that someone else was in the room with her. Only a small reading lamp illuminated her area, the rest of the laboratory being in deep shadow. Then she recognized the caller, and before she could cry out, Jeff shot out a hand and clamped it firmly over her mouth.

'It's all right, Janine,' Jeff whispered as reassuringly as he could. 'Will you promise not to scream and just listen for a minute?'

Janine hesitated, making no move to answer him.

'Do you want to know about Billy?'

Janine nodded vigorously.

'No screams?' insisted Jeff. At her second nod, he released her.

'Where is he?' she blurted out. 'What have you done with him?'

'He's all right,' answered Jeff, fearful that Janine would go back on her promise. 'He's hiding with Digby.'

'What?' It was almost a scream, and Jeff's hand flew to her mouth again. Then seeing she was calmer, he relaxed his grip once more.

'Where are they?' Janine demanded.

'I can't tell you.'

'Why not?'

'Because,' explained Jeff, 'these idiots will try to get Digby.'

'But they think he's a menace,' protested Billy's mother. 'A monster!'

'I know.' Jeff's face became filled with compassion. 'But he's *my* monster now. I love him, and Billy loves him. I'm not letting anyone lay a hand on him until I've done everything I can to save him.'

Janine felt sorry for the young man. She was pleased, too, that her faith in his goodness had not been misplaced. 'But what can you do?'

'The antidote,' Jeff replied firmly.

'We don't know if it works.'

'And I don't have time to find out,' Jeff said, a note of desperation creeping into his voice. 'I can't hide Digby for ever. If the antidote fails okay, so that's the end, but at least I'll have tried. Now, Janine, please. Where is it?'

Janine made up her mind that Jeff's plan could be the only possible solution. She led him to a wall cupboard and opened the doors to reveal a large glass bottle containing a nondescript liquid.

'That's the latest batch,' she told him, but before he could reply another voice bellowed out.

'Ah, ha! Eldon! Got you!'

It was Colonel Masters. He leapt into the room to make a grab for the animal man, but thinking quickly, Jeff thrust back the cupboard door catching the security man full on the nose. Masters staggered back and collapsed in a heap at the laboratory entrance.

'Sorry, Colonel,' Jeff called back as he sped down the corridor, the bottle held firmly in his hand.

Caught in two minds, Janine finally decided to go to Colonel Master's aid and as the man groaned to his senses, she helped him to his feet.

Jeff fled from the administration block, knowing that Masters would soon be in pursuit. As he reached the top of the steps, he saw, through the hazy light of dawn, a familiar figure sitting in a car, waving some keys.

'Clarissa!' exclaimed Jeff in delight. 'Start her up!' And the young man ran to the car as Clarissa inserted the ignition key and made the powerful engine roar into life.

'Stop that man!' came a strangled cry behind them as Jeff edged Clarissa over to the passenger seat. Instantly two soldiers rushed up to grab the Colonel as he made for his own car.

'NO!' bellowed Masters in anger. 'Not me, you fools! Him!' The soldiers released their superior officer and he was soon gunning the engine into life as Janine hurried into the car beside him.

Jeff took stock of the situation as he hurtled the car towards the main gate barrier. He realized at once that he was sitting in General Frank's car, and Clarissa confirmed it, for she was gaily sporting the General's cap. That ridiculous fact helped them through the gate, for in the gloom of dawn, the guard thought Clarissa *was* the General and gave a smart salute as Jeff drove past at tremendous speed.

The chase was on, but in spite of having a full transport unit at his command, Colonel Masters failed to catch Jeff. Instead the unit, completely flummoxed by Jeff's counter instructions via the radio in the General's car, finished up on a bridge over a motorway, not knowing which direction was north and which was up!

Colonel Masters' part in the chase came to an abrupt end when he tried to drive through a narrow gap between two buildings – on his car's side.

So Jeff was able to outdistance the hunters and leave Clarissa in the car while he headed across the rough terrain to the quarry. But, as he ran, he knew he had scored a hollow victory, for the army and Colonel Masters had noted the general direction he was taking.

As he scrambled down the ravine to Billy's side, Jeff knew that it was only a matter of time before they would be caught.

Chapter Twelve

EXIT THE BIGGEST DOG IN THE WORLD

The light aircraft droned like an angry bee, flying high in the clear sky. Jeff glanced up and tried to make himself look as small as possible, for he knew the machine was a spotter plane. Then he chuckled to himself. How ridiculous it was to remain hidden when beside him was a white mountain of a creature that could be seen miles away.

Billy White saw the spotter plane, too, and wiped a tear from his cheek. When would the anti-thing start working? Why was Digby groaning so much? An hour before, he had literally crawled into Digby's mouth and poured the antidote down the dog's mammoth throat. But nothing had happened to reduce his pet's size. Instead, Digby had rolled over to lie against the quarry side whimpering as if in great pain.

The aircraft's pilot radioed his report to the ground where, five miles from the quarry, a cavalcade of infantrymen, troop carriers, jeeps and officers waited for the news.

Colonel Masters turned to Janine with a smile of delighted anticipation. 'They've been spotted,' he told her. 'All three together. It's only a matter of time now.'

The convoy moved in and began to surround the quarry area. Colonel Masters found the army officer in charge of the troops. He picked up a strange-looking, wide-barrelled weapon.

'These the new paralysing gas guns?' he asked, examining the rifle.

'Yes,' replied the officer. 'Knock a man out for up to twenty minutes, depending on the concentration of gas.'

Masters gave the gun an affectionate pat. 'I'll have one,' he muttered, a malicious gleam in his eye. 'I have a personal interest in the matter.'

Suddenly, Colonel Masters received a shock. Coming over the top of the ravine was Jeff Eldon who had decided to make a last effort to stop the army from harming Digby.

'Why don't you pick on someone your own size?' Jeff cried, his anger getting the better of him as he saw the pompous Colonel.

Masters waved back the troops who sprang forward to grab Jeff. 'I'll handle this,' he said, giving the gas gun to the open-mouthed infantry officer and starting to unbuckle his belt.

Taken aback for a moment, Jeff hesitated. Then he put up his fists ready to do battle. But Colonel Masters had no intention of fighting man to man. In a twinkling he had snatched back the gas gun and was pointing it at the advancing Eldon. Instinctively, the young animal man charged forward to defend himself, grappling with Masters. The wrestling match ended quickly as the gun went off, and the Colonel's face froze; then his arms froze, his feet, and his entire body.

With a silly, fixed expression, he keeled over to the ground and lay there, paralysed.

In the confusion that followed, Jeff thought it better to retreat back to the quarry with his friends Billy and Digby. The dog looked in poor shape, panting painfully and giving an occasional groan which brought another tear to Billy's eyes.

'What's wrong with him?' the boy asked, sobbing.

'It's the drug,' Jeff answered solemnly.

'It's not working is it? Digby's still the same size. Is he dying, Jeff?'

Jeff tried to think of an answer which would give the lad new hope, but he had to admit to himself that he had failed to save Digby. A minute later,

General Frank's voice echoed around the ravine giving Jeff a further problem to worry about.

'Eldon,' the General bellowed. 'We know you're in there. Can you hear me?'

Jeff and Billy exchanged glances and the animal man shook his head slowly, then moved slowly up the ravine.

'I can hear you,' he called, aware of the soldiers all around him.

'You are completely surrounded,' General Frank called. 'You cannot escape. The army will commence operations with nerve gas in exactly three minutes. Their orders are to immobilize the dog regardless of whether you stay with it or not. If you wish to risk your own safety that is your affair, but let the boy go. His mother is here.'

Jeff slid thoughtfully down the steep bank. Billy looked sorrowfully into Jeff's eyes.

'I think Digby's dying.'

'Maybe, Billy,' Jeff nodded sombrely. 'But we've got to go.'

Billy seemed to accept the idea, then broke into deep sobs. 'Digby . . . Digby.'

Jeff stood up and helped Billy to his feet. Without speaking, they climbed the slope to the top, leaving the dog lying there in the quarry, panting and groaning.

'Hold your fire,' Jeff shouted at the armed soldiers. 'We're coming out! Come on, Billy.'

The two walked slowly out of the ravine, heads bowed in sorrow, looking tiny against the mass of the quarry landscape. The soldiers sensing their mood, stood silently watching, sentries to the sad scene. Janine White ran forward to clasp her son in a thankful embrace and to provide much needed comfort for the boy's breaking heart. Left alone Jeff strolled past the army officer, empty and beaten.

'All right, men,' said the man in khaki. 'Everybody back. We are withdrawing to a distance of one mile.'

Jeff was pulled up with surprise. 'What's going on?' he asked insistently.

The army man pointed to the distant hills and Jeff, puzzled at first, heard a low rumbling. Then, as the rumble became a roar, and the roar became a scream, his biggest fears were realized.

'No!' he shouted, trying to run back to the quarry. 'You can't!'

'Grab him, men,' ordered the officer, and, helpless with a man pinning each arm, Jeff had to stand and watch as three Royal Air Force jet bombers flew on a screaming low run towards the ravine and Digby.

The bombers were lost to sight over the rim of the quarry slopes, and a series of deafening explosions shook the area as plumes of smoke and flame shot high into the air.

Released by the stunned and straight-faced soldiers, Jeff walked blindly towards where the last stones were falling after the bomb run. The aircraft whined away into the distance and then there was a strange eerie silence.

'Jeff . . . Jeff . . .' Billy's frantic yell broke the spell as the boy came running up to his friend.

'Don't blame them, Billy,' Jeff said sadly. 'I did it. I started it all!'

Putting his arm around the youngster, Jeff strolled quietly away from the soldiers and military equipment. 'I'll get you another dog just like Digby.'

'But he won't be the same as Digby,' Billy protested.

'No,' agreed Jeff, shaking his head. 'He won't be the same, but he'll be very like him and you'll be surprised how quickly you'll forget.'

Jeff suddenly stopped and strained his ears. Did he hear what he thought he heard? No . . . it was the effect of the explosion ringing in his head. But, wait, there it was again . . . a once familiar sound.

Next second, bursting out from a fold in the hills,

a white, shaggy, bounding, barking animal appeared.

'It's Digby!' yelled Billy shrilly.

Jeff stared at the rapidly approaching dog. 'The antidote worked!' he whispered, not daring to believe what his eyes could see. Then he heard a voice from close by. He walked back a pace and saw Janine, her face sad.

'I – I just wanted to say I'm sorry,' she gulped, emotion in her voice.

'It doesn't matter,' laughed Jeff, lightly. 'Look!'

Billy came into view, struggling, cuddling the boisterous, romping dog. 'The antidote worked. Digby's all right!'

Not far away, Colonel Masters lay on a stretcher, his face still set in that stupid expression, his body remaining stiff and inert. Slowly, the effects of the paralysing shot wore off, and the Colonel opened his eyes to blink up at the sky.

An ominous shadow came over him and he blinked again and then sat up. 'Clarissa?' he said, gasping out the word in fearful surprise. Next moment, Masters was charging across the field like a scalded cat. And behind him loped Clarissa, Jeff's chimpanzee. But she had changed. Now she was fifty feet high!

Jeff and Janine heard Masters' petrified shouts

and ran from the rocks to see the gigantic ape. Jeff glanced at Billy's mother and his lips parted in a broad smile.

'Clarissa,' he explained. 'Oh, no! Not again!'

Billy White hugged his beloved Digby, feeling him all over to make certain he was suffering no ill effects after his great ordeal. Billy could hear the shouts of consternation, but he was not worried. It was the problem of those adults. All he knew was that he had his pet back safe and sound. Digby was no longer the biggest dog in the world.